Table of Contents

Introduction

History, as we know it, has long been dominated with the accomplishments of white men as most history books are devoted to educating us about this. Whilst this history is valid and the people written about all played an important part in inventing devices, traditionally they have been viewed as the forefront of championing innovation in western society.

However, what is lesser known is that there were many black individuals who also contributed and helped bring these inventions to life and created their own unique inventions. Unfortunately, this information isn't that well publicised, but we know that black people have long made an impact in culture, technology and society, shaping the world we live in today. This book aims to inform readers of the valuable contribution many black inventors and figures have had on our society and our world as we know it. The inspiring people in this book may not be widely known in mainstream media, however they have changed the world in more ways than one, breaking down racial barriers and giving us inventions that assist us in our daily lives.

Positive black representation is aspirational to children of colour whose history is often ignored in educational learning. This book aims to share the accomplishments of different black figures to enlighten and encourage.

It is easy to read with children and presents lesser known black history in a digestible way with a mixture of newer and older figures highlighted. It also encourages children to think of what career they may have in the future.

"A little bit of knowledge goes a long way" – Khalil Gibran

Samuel Coleridge-Taylor

Black people have been influential in every category of music such rap, hip hop and even classical which has been traditionally associated as a white genre of music. However, there has been a lack of recognised black composers in history.

Samuel Coleridge-Taylor was a respected composer who studied at the royal college of music (in the 1900's) at a time where it wasn't common for black composers to enjoy international success. Coleridge-Taylor (pictured above) broke down barriers with his classical compositions which were revered. He even went on to perform for President Theodore Roosevelt which was an honour and rare event for a man of his background. He was the first black recipient of a blue plaque (a commemorate sign serving as a historical marker), which was erected on his former home in 1975.

Evelyn Dove

Evelyn Dove was a 1920's and 30's jazz singer who studied piano and elocution at the Royal Academy of Music. Dove quickly realised when she graduated that the classical music scene was not welcoming of a mixed-race female singer. However, she was not dissuaded by the discriminatory climate and went on to become the first black singer ever on BBC radio. Dove was broadcast on BBC throughout World War II in a variety of programmes enjoying success and popularity.

Dove (pictured right) helped pave the way for other artists of colour to gain radio airtime and was loved by many listeners, showing that race can transcend the airwaves. Black voices and music have been respected and praised worldwide but the music industry has been hard for black musicians to navigate as they have been met with restrictions and rejections based on their skin colour. They have also been cheated out of proper recognition of their work due to other musicians copying ideas and not crediting them to the original black artist.

Margaret Busby

Years ago, it was hard for writers of colour to get noticed in the literacy world, therefore it was difficult for them to get their work published due to racial barriers and limited opportunities in this sector.

Margaret Busby was Britain's youngest and first black female book publisher in 1967, who in the tough racial climate of the time co – founded the publishers Allison and Busby. This was an inclusive company which welcomed the work of black writers who had previously been ignored. Though A&B did not exclusively publish black authors, it was nevertheless a major catalyst for bringing black literature to the mainstream.

Busby (pictured above) continues to support and encourage young writers to this day, impressed by their enthusiasm and energy! She has written several plays and is a frequent contributor to The Guardian, The Sunday Times and The Independent newspapers.

Jessica Hule

Jessica Hule is a modern inspiration, who also saw a lack of diversity and inclusivity in a commercial market and decided to change it. Spotting a lack of multi-cultural greeting cards in the shops, she rightly observed the need for more diversity in card ranges to reflect the many different races, cultures and religions of consumers thus her business Colour-Blind cards was born in 2006.

The company made history as the first black card range in the UK high street, Clintons, in 2007. Hule (pictured right) was awarded an MBE in 2014, where her contribution to diversity received recognition. Hule understood that representation of different skin colours and races is important to build healthy self-esteem and helps empower children. Therefore, even seeing images on a card that mirror yourself can evoke positive self-image.

Elijah McCoy

Elijah McCoy (pictured left) was a brilliant mechanical inventor who faced injustice and exclusion during his career because of his skin colour. When he tried to get a job as a railroad engineer, the racist management team thought a black man wasn't capable of the job. He was hired to work in the boiler room of trains in the position of a fireman instead.

His parents were former slaves who escaped captivity on the Underground Railroad, so it is interesting that he ended up working on the railroad in later life.

In 1872, McCoy developed and patented an automatic oiling device that lubricated engine parts whilst they were in motion, reducing the need to stop and start the train to apply the process, saving time and money and increasing efficiency. His invention was instantly popular and inspired inferior copycats along the way. Fortunately, McCoy's good reputation proceeded him, and buyers only wanted his original development, bypassing his competitors knock offs and opting for the 'real McCoy'. This phrase is now a well-known expression in the English Language, which highlights how well received his invention was.

Sarah Boone

Boone patented an improvement to the ironing board in 1892, becoming one of the first black women in the US to receive a patent. Her design enabled women's garments and sleeves of clothes to be ironed more efficiently so they looked better. Boone's curved board design made it more convenient to iron shirts and trousers eliminating creases that could occur when ironing garments.

Boone (pictured above) was born enslaved in 1832, going on to marry in 1847. Shortly after, she and her husband were freed under unknown circumstances and moved to Connecticut where she worked as a dressmaker.

Lewis Latimer

Nowadays, no one seems to be without a mobile phone which is great for us to communicate on the go. Before the portable mobile phone, we had landline telephones that are still used in homes, yet less frequently.

I bet you have all heard of Alexander Graham Bell who invented the telephone. However, have you heard of who also played a part in it? Lewis Latimer helped draft the patent for Bell's design of the telephone in 1876. Latimer was sought out by Bell who had created a device and wanted Lewis to draft the drawing necessary for a patent application. Consequently, his important input contributed to the telephone as we know it.

Latimer was a great inventor and in 1881 he patented a carbon filament he had made. This filament is a vital component of the light bulb which is used today in millions of homes around the world! When you switch off your bedroom light before bed, know that Latimer was instrumental in creating it. Latimer devised a way of encasing the filament within a cardboard envelope which prevented the carbon from breaking enabling it to last longer which made it more cost effective for buyers. This facilitated the installation of electric lighting in homes and streets. Involved in the field of incandescent lighting which was a particularly competitive field, Latimer also worked with Hiram Maxim and Edison.

Amazingly, Latimer (pictured above) was even responsible for the early formulation of the air conditioning unit, patenting the forerunner of it in 1886!

Madam C.J. Walker

Madam C.J. Walker was a pioneer in the hair industry, founding her manufacturing company in 1910 and going on to become the first self-made millionaire in America. She invented a line of African American hair care products after suffering with a scalp ailment that caused hair loss. Aware of how important hair is to women, she invested her energy into creating products and selling them around the US.

Walker (pictured above) employed black salespeople who were well trained in cosmetics and well known throughout the black communities as 'walker agents' promoting and advertising. This helped regenerate the modern equivalent of millions of dollars. Her company created career opportunities for black women whose jobs prospects were limited. She also funded scholarships for disadvantaged women, enabling others to gain success of their own. Praised for her philanthropy, her success and business acumen are still admired today.

Annie Malone

Around the same time, Annie Malone was also an entrepreneur in this industry and accumulated great wealth by developing a chemical product that straightened black hair without damaging it. Interestingly, she even gave Walker her first job as a hair care sales agent. She also created and patented the pressing comb in 1920 which is still in circulation today.

Malone (pictured right) faced struggles in securing sales of her product, because as a black woman she was blocked from accessing traditional distribution routes. Malone was committed to social welfare, giving back to her community by building Poro College. This college lent itself as a hub for African Americans who were denied access to other entertainment venues due to segregation.

Mary Davidson Kenner

Mary Davidson Kenner was a very creative lady who was the brains behind many practical inventions that have helped make peoples everyday lives easier. You know when you go the toilet in a restaurant and use the tissue paper from its holder? She made that in 1982! An invention that is used today in commercial places and business buildings around the world, something that be viewed as insignificant aids people in the simplest way – Genius!

Kenner (pictured below) drew inspiration from her daily life. When her sister Mildred developed multiple sclerosis and had to use a walking frame, she patented a serving tray that could be attached to the frame. This allowed Mildred to carry things around with her. Another practical invention of hers was a back washer that could be attached to the wall of a shower to help people clean hard-to-reach parts of their back.

Kenner eventually held five patents to her name – more than any other African American woman in history which was an amazing feat. Some of Kenner's earlier inventions such as feminine products were held back for years due to racial discrimination. Companies even terminated working with her after discovering she was black. However, she remained undeterred as she was motivated by the love of creating. Subsequently, she never reaped the financial rewards of her inventions and didn't become rich like other inventors.

Have you ever saw something that needs fixing and thought of a solution? You can use those ideas to create inventions that could one day become staples in society! Kenner believed that anyone could become an inventor if they put their mind to it and explored their abilities.

Frederick McKinley Jones

Frederick McKinley Jones was one of the most prolific black inventors who patented over 60 inventions, most being in the field of refrigeration. It can be said he pioneered the fridge as we know and use today.

In 1935, Jones invented a solution to prevent ice melting during long haul road transportation of food by developing a roof insulated cooling system to ensure food stayed fresh. So, when we eat food straight out of the fridge chilled at the right temperature, we can thank Jones for that. This invention is invaluable to society and a staple in our homes as it ensures food preservation, therefore its importance cannot be denied.

Developing a knack for mechanics early in life, Jones built a transmitter needed to broadcast programming for his towns local radio station. He also developed a device to combine moving pictures with sound in the late 1920's as he explored electronics.

Jones (pictured above) also invented box office equipment that gave out tickets for shows and returned change to customers, again ahead of its time and again another product we use today on our cinema and theatre trips. This invention is one we use without consideration, yet it undoubtedly makes the process run smoother for the customer and the organisation. Awarded the National Medal of Technology in 1991, he became the first black inventor to receive such a prestigious honour.

Thomas Elkins

In 1879, Thomas Elkins (pictured right) patented an improved fridge design to preserve perishable food enabling it to last longer showing that great minds think alike! However, Elkin's design was also made to chill human dead bodies which a was challenging problem at the time – gross but true!

In 1872, Elkins also patented his design for an improved chamber commands – the toilet to you and me.

His design combined a washstand, table, mirror and chamber stool paving the way for the bathroom/ toilet as we know it with its added accompaniments – this makes toilet usage more comfortable and practical. So, when we are using extra facilities in the toilet in its modernised form, remember that this was Elkin's original vision.

Alfred .L. Cralle

Do you love ice cream? I guarantee you've seen an ice cream scoop used to scoop it out. Alfred .L. Cralle invented this, something that seems insignificant but has benefitted people to get ice cream in equal measures. And who doesn't want the right amount of ice cream?!

Whilst working at a hotel, Cralle came up with the idea of the scoop when he observed servers struggling to get the sufficient amount into their cone.

Cralle (pictured right) thought of a solution to this and patented and created a mechanical device in 1897. This device was designed to scoop up ice cream and other food without it sticking. The scoop was cheap, durable and easy to use and quickly become a popular product. Unfortunately, Cralle did not become well known for his invention as it was easily copied and adapted. However, he remained a successful business promoter and investor, advocating black enterprises.

Otis Boykin

Did you know that Otis Boykin (pictured left) made a notable contribution to science in 1959? Boykin made his impact by improving the circuits in pacemakers – a device that replaces parts of the heart to keep it working and beating at a normal pace, making it a scientific breakthrough. His adaption of a control unit made it safer to use in people's bodies, eliminating wider risks and has saved countless lives. The patented wire precision resistor allowed determined amounts of electrical currents to flow for a specific purpose, safely controlling its output.

In 1961, Boykin refined his invention and created an electrical resistor that was inexpensive to manufacture and straightforward to reproduce. This was an immense breakthrough that allowed many electronic devices to be made cheaper with increased reliability and has been used in products ranging from IBM computers to military missiles. His invention is much appreciated, however not as widely celebrated as it should be.

Daniel Hale Williams

Daniel Hale Williams (pictured left) was a pioneering doctor and opened the first medical facility in America to have interactional staff in 1891. This was an amazing feat as this was a time of segregation of races and Jim Crow laws which denied racial equality and restricted black rights. Due to discrimination, African Americans were barred from being admitted to hospitals, limiting their access to health care, with black doctors being refused secure staff positions. Williams objected to this and with the opening of his Provident hospital, he challenged these rules and introduced a fully integrated staff base.

In 1893, Williams made history again when he successfully performed open heart surgery on a patient, becoming one of the first doctors in the world to do so. Williams is remembered as a pioneering physician and an advocate for medical African American representation.

Lonnie Johnson

Lonnie Johnson worked for NASA and has earned numerous awards for his spacecraft control systems; however, he is best known and loved for inventing the Super Soaker in 1989. You know that play gun you fill up with water and spray on all your friends and chase them around with in the summer? Well he created it! How amazing and how fun! Johnson got the inspiration whilst he was working on an eco-friendly heat pump, as he was aware of the need for environmental sustainability, therefore you could say his invention was a happy accident! The super soaker has gone on to be one of the top selling toys in the world!

Johnson has enjoyed tremendous success and brought pleasure to children (and adults!) worldwide. He has patented over 100 patents on different products and processes including a toy rocket launcher, heat pumps and a ceramic battery. He even invented a wet diaper detector which played a nursery rhyme when full, but this failed to catch on.

Johnson (pictured above) struggled for years to find a company willing to see his vision and invest in his idea to gain commercial success, but once it hit the market, sales soared! However, it has been said there were some complications regarding patents with the Super Soaker and accompanying rumours stated Johnson missed out on profits for invention due to legal disputes. Fortunately, he has retained ownership of his invention and continues to receive royalties for it to this day.

Acknowledged for his ground-breaking scientific work and inventions, Johnson was inducted into the State of Alabama Engineering Hall of Fame in 2011.

Valerie Thomas

Like Johnson, Valerie Thomas also worked at NASA and is best known for her patented illusion transmitter. The inspiration came after she saw a creation at an exhibition which included an illusion of a light bulb that was alight, even though it had been removed from its socket making it impossible to really be lit. The illusion, which involved another light bulb and concave mirrors gave Thomas  the idea to incorporate it into her work. This resulted in experiments where she observed how the position of a concave mirror would affect the real object that it reflected. Using this technology, she invented the illusion transmitter which was patented in 1980. NASA continues to use this device today as it multifunctional and has been adapted for use in surgery and the production of TV screens. This was the premise for modern 3D technology.

Thomas (pictured above) enjoyed a long successful career at NASA and contributed widely to the study of space. She helped to develop computer program designs that supported research on Halley's Comet, the ozone layer, and satellite technology. In the 1970s, she managed the development of the image-processing systems for Landsat, the first satellite to send images to the Earth from space, an amazing achievement! Her interest in science was not encouraged until her later years and this lack of initial support in her studies inspired her to reach out to students to motivate them to pursue their goals!

Marsai Martin

Marsai Martin (pictured right) is a young actress who is making history with her achievements in film. In 2019, she starred in "Little" for Universal Pictures in the leading role. At just 13 years old, Martin was named an executive producer for the film, making her the youngest in history. The film was a success, grossing over $50 million at the box office, how awesome! Her contribution to cinematography has been already begun to receive recognition and she has garnered  nominations at the NAACP Image Awards, BET Awards and SAG Awards.

Philip Emeagwali

We've all heard of Steve Jobs who created the iconic iPhone, but have you heard of Philip Emeagwali? He was forced to drop out of school aged 14 due to lack of funds but that didn't stand in his way in becoming one of the top computer pioneers of our modern times. Emeagwali (pictured right) has been dubbed the Bill Gates of Africa, although he is famous in his own right! Inspired by nature which sparked his study into bees, this led to a great discovery – the construction of the honeycomb was similar to that of a computer processor which could be improved to work more efficiently.

In 1989, a time where technology was still in its early stages, he put his idea into place by using 65,000 processes to invent the first supercomputer in the world! This computer was able to perform 3.1 billion calculations per second, a phenomenal feat at its time.

Lisa Gelobter

Do you like the GIF? Of course, you do, everyone does! It's those funny crazy moving pictures used to convey reactions that are so popular to use on social media. Lisa Gelobter (pictured right) helped create this phenomenon as she laid the early groundwork for the program by developing the animation used to produce it in the 1980's.

Gelobter has been integrally involved with pioneering internet technologies such as Shockwave which formed the beginning of web animation. She also played a significant role in the emergence of the online video through Hulu. So, if you think you could create the next internet craze, go ahead! You never know, it just might go viral! Using her background in design, engineering and product management to impact and influence how we consume media, Gelobter is one of the first black women to ever raise $1 million in venture capital funding. This showcases her business acumen and creative talents alike.

Charles Harrison

Charles Harrison was an industrial designer who created the view-master toy which was a photography device that allowed viewers to see images in 3D. This was revolutionary for the era (1950's). The remodelling of this item in 1958 turned it into a popular children's toy which was accessible to all and provided instant fun and amazement.

Harrison had many challenges in his career as some companies refused to hire him because he was black. However, he preserved and spent 30 years developing over 700 consumer products which are still household items today and are probably things we take for granted. Have you used a see-through measuring cup in science or cooking? Harrison made it. Seen a ride on lawn mower? Harrison contributed to its formation.

Harrison (pictured above) is also credited with pioneering the plastic rubbish bin from its original clunky model to the more manageable portable type we see today on wheels. Improving the quality and efficiency of the tasks we perform in everyday life; Harrison's designs did not require extensive instructions. He struggled with dyslexia and subsequently wanted his products to be used universally with ease.

Harrison created a variety of household goods ranging from toasters, portable hair dryers, shoe buffers and baby cribs whilst working at Sears designing firm, where he became the company's first African American executive.

He also created a travel sized sewing machine in 1978 which lead to collaborations with designers from the UK and Japan. His unwavering commitment to the needs of the average consumer is showcased in the extraordinary breadth and innovation of his product designs.

Garrett Morgan

Garrett Morgan, like many inventors in this book, created early versions of items that are in circulation today. Morgan became interested in machinery through textile jobs. In 1914 (the year World War I started) he invented what was known as a 'safety hood' that helped air become more breathable. Due to the ongoing war, this was an early version of a gas mask that protected soldiers from poisonous gas and added protection during bomb zones to stop the inhalation of harmful chemicals.

Morgan encountered resistance to his devices from some consumers, as racial tensions remained despite advancements in African American rights. To counteract this, Morgan hired a white actor to pretend to be the inventor during presentations of his breathing device which fooled the public and secured the sales he needed.

Exhibiting more of his brilliance, Morgan established the Cleveland Call newspaper in 1920. He also made an oil hair dye and curved-tooth comb to straight African American hair which garnered great success. This gave him financial security and flexibility to pursue his more complicated time-consuming inventions.

Showing no end to his intelligence and ingenuity, in 1922, Morgan (pictured above) filed a patent for his traffic signal which included 3 signals which indicated to drivers to use caution and awareness. Morgan's traffic light system prevented millions of accidents and encouraged safety practices on the road. When you are waiting for the lights to change from amber (which is now used instead of yellow which was used when it was first invented), remember Morgan's innovation lead the way to road safety procedures.

Morgan's work provided the blueprint for many important advancements in engineering and serves as a basis for research conducted by modern-day inventors.

Alexander Miles

In 1884, Miles (pictured right) built a three-story brownstone building in Duluth which became known as the Miles Block. Whilst using an elevator with his young daughter, Miles was alarmed at the risk associated with an elevator shaft door left ajar. This motivated him to draft his design for automatically opening and closing elevator doors which was patented in 1887.

His invention attached a flexible belt to the elevator cage, which adjusted between floors, allowing the elevator shaft doors to operate at the appropriate times, reducing hazards and accidents. Now a standard feature of elevator doors, his mechanism ensures safety and protection.
In Chicago,1900, Miles created an insurance agency with the goal of eliminating discriminatory treatment of African Americans to help their financial advancement. Noted for his exceptional engineering, Miles was inducted into the National Inventors Hall of Fame in 2007.

Lyda .D. Newman

Lyda .D. Newman (pictured left) was only 14 when she invented her modified version of the hairbrush. Her experience with her own hair prompted her to develop an improved version. She was also the third black women to ever receive a patent in 1898. Newman's version of the hairbrush included synthetic bristles, as opposed to animal hair which was the material commonly used. This made the brush more durable as synthetic lasted longer and could also withstand water much better. Another notable feature she added to simplify the cleaning process was detachable bristles. These significant modifications made the hairbrush more affordable to everyone and is similar of the plastic brushes used today.

Newman was an activist for women's rights to vote and participate in office. She was also a main organiser of the African American branch of the Women's Suffrage Party, working closely with other prominent white suffragists and was an instrumental part in the movement. The goal was to empower all women.

Marie Van Britton Brown

Marie Van Britton Brown invented the first home security system in 1966 and has provided inspiration for the modern home security systems used around the world today. Concerned by rising crime rates in her area, Brown sought to create a system that informed her of a break in but also simultaneously alerted the authorities straight away in order to catch the criminals and keep her family safe, as quickly as possible.

This was revolutionary. Her original invention comprised of peepholes to spot perpetrators, a camera, a 2-way microphone and a very important part of the design, an alarm button that contacted police immediately. Showing tremendous innovation, the design also had a voice component allowing her to talk to the person outside her house. The door could be unlocked through remote control to let the person in if they weren't a threat, enhancing protection.

Browns invention was well received and recognised for its brilliance, winning an award from the National Scientists Committee.

Brown (pictured above) is also credited with inventing one of the first closed circuit televisions! Brown's security system brought the of CCTV into the home. This has expanded with lots of elements of Browns original design still in operation, confirming it has stood the test of time. Today this technology is installed in millions of buildings, offices and home throughout the globe.

Something to think about...

Do you love to sing and make music like Samuel Coleridge-Taylor and Evelyn Dove?

Music can be a real career that allows you to use your voice/sound to brighten up someone's day.

Music is a very broad subject; therefore, you could become a singer, play an instrument for a band or even create your own music for adverts or film productions. Music reaches beyond just singing tunes though. You could write your own songs and own the copyright to them so you could earn royalties every time your jam is played on the radio!

Are you interested in writing, literacy and stories like Margaret Busby?

If so, you could become an author and write your own book one day! Most films are based on books, so after writing a novel, potentially it could be turned into a blockbuster movie on the big screen! If you love weaving worlds on paper and creating characters and scenarios, writing a book could turn from a fun hobby to a legitimate career.

Have you ever spotted something missing on the shelves in the shops you visit or wished you could buy an item that doesn't exist?

Well you could create your own product to fill that gap! Just like Jessica Hule, Madam C.J. Walker and Annie Malone did.

Designing your own product can be a flow of ideas or one bright spark. However, if it feels like a light bulb moment, it's worth pursuing and trying to develop. It could be the next best thing!

Could you put your thinking cap on to invent devices that help people's lives in any way possible, like Lewis Latimer and Elijah McCoy did?

Any invention for any purpose is amazing so whatever you decide to create will be valuable as that's the beauty of inventions – there will always be someone, somewhere who wants it or need its! You just have to find the market you want to channel your energy into! Investigate areas that interest you. Research how to turn your idea into a viable product.

Could you think of a device to promote safety or aid security like Alexander Miles or Marie Van Britton Brown?

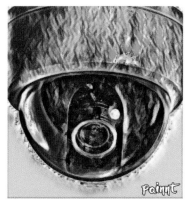

Big or small, if it can solve a problem, help ease menial tasks or inspire new ways of completing chores then it could be just what buyers are looking for! Once the idea is there, you can elaborate on it by building a prototype and testing it out in real life. You don't need fancy equipment, use what you can find and see how it goes! Experimentation is key to see what works.

Could you invent a new household staple like Frederick McKinley Jones and Thomas Elkins?

Designing can be fun and it's all about trial and error – some things may work; others may fall flat. Tweaking and trimming your ideas can eventually lead to one that is the money maker, the ground breaker! It is good to focus on one or two industries you are interested so you can really hone your skills/ideas in these areas.

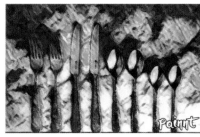

Take inspiration from Mary Davidson, Alfred .L. Cralle and Sarah Boone.

Drawing pictures of your concept then thinking how to bring it to life through implementation can be challenging yet rewarding once you see your creation completed. Sketching your idea helps you see how it will look and see what supplies you would need to manufacture it. Keep a notepad to hand to jot down creative thoughts.

Do you aspire to be like Otis Boykin or Daniel Hale Williams?

If so, you could be a doctor, a nurse or even a surgeon who operates on

people to save lives! A career in medicine requires dedication and commitment. You would need to go to medical school to train and understand how the body works in order to solve health issues but all the hard work and studying would pay off as you would become an integral part of making people better which makes for a fulfilling career.

Could you be the next big toy creator like Charles Harrison or Lonnie Johnson?

You could even own your own version of Toys R Us! Making toys brings endless joy to children around the world so if you have an idea of something you think a child would like to play with, be it playdoh or pirates, get creating!

It is very important to patent your ideas to protect them. This ensures you rightfully receive profit if they sell and it also secures ownership of them legally. That way, no one else can steal it and pass it off as their own.

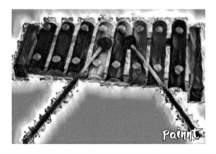

Are you into computers like Philip Emeagwali?

If so, you could discover a very interesting career in this industry that is constantly evolving. There is a demand for jobs in this sector from coding, constructing video games to cyber security. If you are more into software creation like Lisa Gelobter, use your mind today to create the gadgets/ apps of tomorrow!

Are you passionate about protecting and progressing human rights for equality for all people like Lyda .D. Newman was? You could be an activist campaigning for change or work for charities and organisations that are dedicated to helping others.

Does the concept of space fascinate you like Valerie Thomas? You can explore space and learn more on the internet, visit museums to expand your knowledge and maybe even apply for NASA's recruitment programs to train to be an astronaut! Or if you are into films like Marsai Martin? You could produce films, become a director or act onscreen or stage. You would need to practice lines and audition for roles but who knows, we may see you on the silver screen one day!

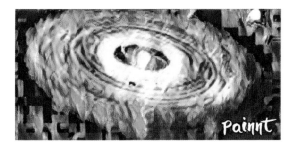

Hopefully learning all this information has inspired you.

These wonderful people are aspirations and show that you can achieve anything.

You can overcome setbacks and adversities that may come into your path, as long as you stay focused and positive. Armed with knowledge, education and ambition you can succeed in whatever career you choose!

Never give up and always follow your dreams!

Maybe one day we see you top the book/pop charts or see invention out there to buy. Whether it be on the toy aisle or electronics is your choice!

Thank you for reading!

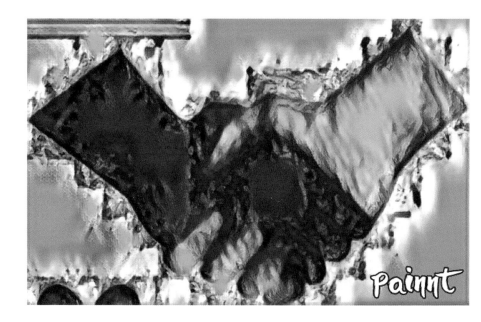

Who has inspired you the most in this book and why?

Drawings by Aaliyah Raybone (aged 8)

References

Images of individuals featured: Sourced from Google in the public domain

Digital art of images: Tamsy Ashman

www.bbc.co.uk

www.biography.com

www.blackhistory.com

www.blackhistorymonth.org.uk

www.britannica.com

www.edtrust.org

www.face2faceafrica.com

www.forbes.com

www.histarch.illinois.edu

www.independent.co.uk

www.myblackhistory.net

www.myblackpast.org

www.nsbp.org

www.peoplepill.co.uk

www.stylist.co.uk

www.teacher.scholastic.com

www.thinkgrowth.org

www.thoughtco.com

www.wenta.co.uk

www.yesmagazine.com

Printed in Poland
by Amazon Fulfillment
Poland Sp. z o.o., Wrocław

61406069R00016